Abuela's Gift

by Isabel Sendao
illustrated by Durga Bernhard

Scott Foresman
is an imprint of

Glenview, Illinois • Boston, Massachusetts • Chandler, Arizona
Upper Saddle River, New Jersey

Lupe ran home from the school bus stop. It was the last day of classes before winter break, and she was very excited about her family trip. She was going to Mexico to visit her grandmother for Christmas. It had been a whole year since she had seen her *abuela*, which means grandmother in Spanish. The trip was always fun for Lupe because she got to practice her Spanish and visit many different fun places in Mexico. She also got to spend time with her cousins and hear stories about when her mother was a little girl.

Lupe's family lived in Phoenix, Arizona. Her abuela lived in northern Mexico, a short distance from Phoenix. Every year at Christmas Lupe's family drove to see Abuela.

Lupe loved the drive. She would pack the trunk with gifts for her cousins, aunts, and uncles. The gift that she got for Abuela was always the most special. Lupe would spend lots of time thinking about it. She missed her Abuela greatly and wanted to make sure she knew how much she loved her.

The Christmas celebration was important in Lupe's family. It was the only time of year that they got to see Abuela. That made Lupe put even more effort into selecting her abuela's present.

This year, Lupe had decided that her Christmas gift to Abuela would be a special book of recipes. She wanted to show her gratitude for all the wonderful times she had spent cooking dishes in Abuela's kitchen. Lupe had worked hard to write down each recipe using her best handwriting. Next to each entry she had added a photograph. Each photograph showed Lupe at home holding up the dish that she had prepared from each recipe.

Lupe had had a fun time putting together her special book of recipes. Every week she cooked something new from her recipe collection. Every week she had her mother take a picture of her in front of her latest creation. Lupe was astonished at how well her book had turned out.

For Lupe, the best part of visiting Abuela was the time they spent together in the kitchen. Abuela's kitchen was a very special place. There were always wonderful smells wafting around in it. And you could always find a variety of delicious Mexican treats tucked away here and there.

As much as Lupe liked those things, what she cherished most of all about her time in Abuela's kitchen were the hours when Abuela would tell her stories about Mexico. For as long as Lupe could remember, Abuela had told her stories. The stories had become family tradition.

Another family tradition involved the baking of the Rosca de Reyes. Rosca de Reyes is a pastry. Made from sweet bread, it is twisted into a round braid and decorated with candied fruits. The fruits and round braid make it look like a king's crown.

In Mexico, the Rosca de Reyes is made to celebrate the sacred Festival of the Three Kings, which happens twelve days after Christmas. The Rosca de Reyes is always the centerpiece of the Mexican holiday dinner table.

In years past, Lupe had not been old enough to help bake the Rosca de Reyes. This year would be different. Abuela and Lupe's mother knew that Lupe was now ready to help with the baking. It was difficult to make. But Lupe's mother had learned how to make the Rosca de Reyes when she was Lupe's age, as had Abuela. So now was the time!

You couldn't make Rosca de Reyes without telling the story of the Three Kings. It was a story that Lupe had heard many times. Twelve days after Christmas, on January 6, people in Mexico celebrate the procession of the Three Kings, Caspar, Melchior, and Balthasar. These three kings had brought gifts of gold, frankincense, and myrrh to the baby Jesus. In Mexico, January 6 is the day set aside for the distribution of the childrens' Christmas gifts.

On the eve of the festival, Mexican children leave their shoes on the windowsill. They fill the shoes with hay for the kings' camels. This ensures that the camels are happy and that the kings will leave the children gifts. Lupe always left her shoe on the windowsill, hoping to please the camels.

Lupe enjoyed the procession of the Three Kings. At times she felt sad, because so few families in Phoenix celebrated the wonderful holiday. But here in Mexico, Abuela's entire community took part in the event. It made Lupe feel like she was connected to something special.

As soon as Lupe entered Abuela's home, memories of all the previous Christmas celebrations came rushing back to her. The smell of Abuela's famous hot chocolate filled the air, blending with the sweet smell of the wood stove. Lupe could hardly contain her excitement as she said hello to everyone and unpacked all of the gifts she had brought.

Lupe sat down by the hearth afterwards. This was another of her favorite activities at Abuela's house. The hearth had a wonderful smell that was nearly as good as that of the hot chocolate. Lupe loved to stare at its glowing coals and soak up their warmth.

After a while the hearth became too warm to sit by. So Lupe got up and bounced into the warm and inviting kitchen, following the scent of the chocolate. Abuela stood waiting in the kitchen. She knew that her granddaughter would show up there eventually!

Lupe said to Abuela, "I could smell the chocolate as soon as I entered the house!" Abuela smiled. She said, "I had remembered how much you liked my hot chocolate. So I prepared some for you, along with another of your favorite treats. Try some!"

Abuela handed Lupe a steaming mug of hot chocolate and a *churro*. *Churros* are made of dough and covered in sugar and cinnamon. They had a crispy, crunchy taste that Lupe found irresistible. And dunking them in Abuela's hot chocolate only made them better!

Lupe finished her treat. Soon after Abuela asked Lupe to go with her to the market. They needed to pick up ingredients for the Rosca de Reyes. Lupe lost no time in getting ready. She told her mother that she was going out and grabbed her notebook along with Abuela's basket.

Lupe always carried her little notebook around when she was cooking with Abuela. She took notes to make sure that she didn't miss anything. Lupe wrote down exactly which ingredients were used and in what amounts. She even wrote down where she bought everything. That way, she could go shopping on her own some day at Abuela's market!

The outdoor market was buzzing with activity. It seemed as if everyone in town was there. There were brightly colored Christmas decorations everywhere. Here and there stood equally colorful displays advertising the different foods. Phoenix had nothing that could compare to the market. Because of this Lupe was sad whenever the shopping was done.

Lupe loved to wander up and down the market's aisles smelling the wonderful scents of the fruits, spices, fish, breads, and meats. Best of all, Lupe could try out her Spanish with the vendors. Lupe's Spanish was already good. But she knew she could always use more practice!

Lupe and Abuela made their way to the fruit and nut stand. There Abuela picked out the candied fruit she needed for the Rosca de Reyes. Lupe could never get enough of the fruits' amazing colors. Many of them shimmered with a thick coating of sugar. Lupe couldn't wait to try them all!

Abuela took out her purse to pay. As she did the fruit vendor said, "Remember to get the baby Jesus. I recommend the bakery down the street." Lupe didn't understand what he meant. Abuela explained that a small figure of the baby Jesus is usually baked into the Rosca de Reyes. Whoever finds the figure in their piece has to host the next holiday party.

"It works like a lottery," Abuela described. "Everyone at the dinner table gets very excited about it. It adds more fun to the tradition."

Abuela visited the bakery on the way home. There she bought two of the baby Jesus figures. Lupe placed them into the basket. Then she slipped her hand into Abuela's for the walk back to her house.

Abuela and Lupe made one last stop on the way home to buy spices. Lupe felt like she was carrying around a basket full of treasures. She couldn't wait to start cooking!

The next morning, Abuela and Lupe got to work right away on baking the Rosca de Reyes. Abuela read the ingredients out loud. Lupe carefully wrote them down in her notebook. Then she measured them out and put them into the bowl. Later on Lupe's mother joined them to help prepare the rest of the meal.

While they were cooking together Lupe's mother talked about what it was like when Abuela had taught her how to bake Rosca de Reyes. Then Abuela told the story of how *her* mother had taught her how to bake Rosca de Reyes.

Hearing these stories made Lupe feel special. She saw how she was connected to a tradition that stretched back way beyond Abuela. Abuela's and her mother's stories made it sound like the family had been baking Rosca de Reyes since the beginning of time!

While they cooked, the rest of the family sat around in the living room, catching up on what they had been doing over the past year. Now and then Lupe's cousins would visit the kitchen to chat with her. At times they could be a little wild, but at Christmas they made sure to be on their best behavior.

Lupe loved to see her family so happy together. She felt proud that she was old enough to share responsibility for making the family meal.

Lupe's mother finished making the rest of the meal and helped serve the dinner with Lupe and Abuela. Lupe listened to the adults' conversation while she ate. They talked about the differences between life in Mexico and life in the United States. Lupe knew it was difficult to have the family living in two different countries. But she knew that they handled it as best they could.

The family finished eating dinner. At last it was time for dessert! Lupe helped bring all kinds of sweets out to the table. Lupe's mother had prepared her famous *flan*, a rich and dense egg custard. Her aunt had prepared *arroz con leche*, a type of rice pudding. There was more of the steaming hot chocolate and cinnamon-covered *churros*.

Finally, Lupe carried in the Rosca de Reyes. It looked beautiful! Its golden brown crust was sprinkled in sugar and covered in clusters of candied fruits. Lupe had worked hard on the pastry. Everyone at the table gave her compliments on how well she had done baking it. Lupe beamed.

Abuela made sure that each person took a generous slice. Lupe's mother found the baby Jesus in her piece. That meant she would have the honor of hosting the next holiday party! Everyone congratulated Lupe's mother for her good luck.

The family sat around the dinner table talking for a while after dessert. Then they moved over to the living room to exchange Christmas gifts. Soon it was Lupe's turn to run and get Abuela her gift.

Suddenly shy, Lupe presented Abuela with the recipe book that she had made. Everyone fell silent as Lupe explained how she made it, describing all the different notes she had to take down in her notebook in order to get the recipes just right. Lupe also talked about how much she enjoyed Abuela's storytelling and cooking.

Abuela's wrinkled face broke into a big smile. She held Lupe close as she leafed through the pages, showing everyone the photos. In each one Abuela could see that Lupe had worked hard to get the recipes prepared exactly right.

"What a beautiful book!" Abuela said. "And what a wonderful way to remember our recipes. Now if you'll just wait a minute, I have a gift for you."

Abuela excused herself and disappeared into her bedroom. She returned a few moments later holding a very big and very old-looking book in her hands. Abuela explained that it was the greatest gift she ever received. It was a family scrapbook that Lupe's great-great-grandmother had started when she was a little girl. She had passed it down to Abuela when she thought the time was right. Now Abuela was passing it down to Lupe!

Abuela opened the book and started turning the pages, showing them to the family as she went. They saw old, yellowed wedding invitations and photographs from past holiday parties. Lupe noticed her own birth announcement and a picture of her on the first day of kindergarten. At the very back of the book there was a carefully drawn family tree that went back for many generations. Abuela closed the book and held it out to Lupe.

Looking seriously into her granddaughter's eyes, she said, "This book is yours now, but it comes with an important responsibility. Now you are in charge of keeping our traditions alive. My gift to you will become your gift to the rest of the family as you record our history for years to come."

That Christmas in Mexico was one Lupe would remember for the rest of her life. She spent the entire drive back to Phoenix thinking about the gift that Abuela had given her. She felt honored to be trusted with the responsibility of keeping the family traditions alive. But she also was a little scared. What if she couldn't do well at her new task?

Lupe's mother reassured her that she could.

"Think about all the hard work you put into learning the recipes from Abuela," she said.

Lupe smiled as she stared out of the car window, imagining all the stories and recipes she would add to her great-great-grandmother's special book.

Different Countries, Different Gifts

Different cultures have different traditions of gift-giving. In China, gift-giving is surrounded by etiquette and ceremony. There are certain days when gifts are required, such as birthdays and weddings. It is considered rude not to offer a gift on these days.

Gift-giving takes place on January 6 during the Mexican celebration of Christmas. Some Mexican children receive gifts on both Christmas Day and January 6. This is due to the influence that the American Christmas celebration has had in Mexico.

In both the Mexican and Chinese cultures, gifts represent the respect and admiration that the benefactor has for the person receiving his or her gift. What do you feel like when you receive a gift?

Traditional Chinese wedding gifts